NOW YOU CAN READ.....
JOSEPH AND HIS BROTHERS

STORY RETOLD BY LEONARD MATTHEWS

ILLUSTRATED BY HARRY BISHOP

Published by Rourke Publications, Inc., P.O. Box 3328, Vero Beach, Florida 32964. Copyright © 1984 by Rourke Publications, Inc. All copyrights reserved. No part of this book may be reproduced in any form without written permission from the publisher. Printed in the United States of America.

The Publishers acknowledge permission from Brimax Books for the use of the name "Now You Can Read" and "Large Type For First Readers" which identify Brimax Now You Can Read series.

Library of Congress Cataloging in Publication Data

Matthews, Leonard.
  Joseph and his brothers.

  (Now you can read—Bible stories)
  Summary: Retells the Bible story of Joseph, whose brothers tried to kill him because of his dreams.
  1. Joseph (Son of Jacob)—Juvenile literature.
2. Bible. O.T.—Biography—Juvenile literature.
3. Bible stories, English—O.T. Genesis. [1. Joseph (Son of Jacob) 2. Bible stories—O.T.] I. Title.
II. Series.
BS580.J6M38 1984 222'.11'0924 [B] 84-15126
ISBN 0-86625-311-4

GROLIER ENTERPRISES CORP.

JOSEPH AND HIS BROTHERS

There was once a boy whose name was Joseph. His father was Jacob. Jacob had twelve sons in all. Ten of them were older than Joseph. They did not like Joseph. One brother was younger than Joseph. His name was Benjamin. He liked Joseph and the two boys often played together.

Joseph was a smart boy and the favorite of his father Jacob. As they grew older, all the brothers helped to look after the sheep and the cattle that their father Jacob owned. Only Joseph wanted to do more than that. He did not want to work on a farm all his life. He wanted to be something more than just a farmer. He started to teach himself about other subjects. He always worked hard.

At this time little Benjamin was not yet old enough to work with his brothers in the fields. Often Joseph would sit with his father, listening well to everything that Jacob told him. Jacob saw that one day Joseph would be a great man. That was one reason why he was so proud of him.

Joseph's ten older brothers were not like him at all. They did not listen to their father. They were clumsy and careless.

They often made mistakes. Somehow Joseph was always there to tell his brothers where they had gone wrong.

Joseph's ten brothers did not thank him for pointing out their mistakes. They hated him.

They hated him even more when he spoke to their father about the mistakes they were making.

They often talked to each other about Joseph. They thought Joseph was a spy, always running to his father to tell tales about them. In fact, Joseph was hoping Jacob would teach them how to do things the right way.

Joseph had two dreams. He told his brothers about them. He said that his dreams meant that someday Joseph would rule over his brothers.

His brothers did not like hearing this. Matters went from bad to worse when Jacob gave Joseph a new coat. It was a beautiful coat. It had long sleeves. It was striped with many bright colors.

Joseph's ten brothers were very jealous. They wished that they had a coat like Joseph's. They also wished never to see Joseph again.

Their chance came one day when they were all working in the fields. By now Jacob knew that they might not be doing their work well.

He asked Joseph to go and make sure that all was right with his brothers. Joseph was wearing his coat of many colors at the time.

The ten brothers saw Joseph coming toward them. "Here he comes again to watch what we are doing," growled Reuben, the eldest. "Yes and he is wearing that new coat of his," cried another brother named Judah.

"If only he would go away and never return," said a third brother. Judah looked at Reuben. "We could do something about that," he said.

Reuben shrugged his shoulders. "And what could we do?" he asked. Judah pulled out a knife.

Reuben understood at once what his brother Judah meant. He shook his head. "No, we must not kill our brother," he said. Then he thought for a few moments.

Then Reuben said quickly, "Let us take Joseph into the desert. There we will throw him into a pit and leave him."

All the other brothers thought that this was a good idea. As soon as Joseph came near, they jumped on him. They tied him hand and foot. Then, they dragged him away.

In spite of his struggles, they dragged him far into the desert.

When they found a deep pit, they threw him into it and left him there.

On their way home the ten brothers met some traders riding camels. They were heading south toward the land of Egypt. As they drew near, Judah smiled.

"I have just had a great idea," he told Reuben. "This is what we will do with Joseph."

"We will sell Joseph to the traders," said Judah. They would take him to Egypt as a slave.

The other brothers agreed to the plan. So Joseph was sold as a slave.

Judah poured some goat's blood over Joseph's coat.

"Now we will tell father we found it," he said. "He will think some wild animals have killed Joseph."

When Jacob saw the coat he was heart broken. The brothers thought they would never see Joseph again. When they did meet again, Joseph was the governor of Egypt.

All these appear in the pages of the story. Can you find them?

Jacob

traders

Reuben

Benjamin

Judah

Joseph

Now tell the story in your own words.